ALICIA SHEVETONE

food WITH SPIRIT

ALCOHOL-INFUSED RECIPES

GAUDIUM

Gaudium Publishing

Las Vegas • Chicago • Palm Beach

Published in the United States of America by
Histria Books
7181 N. Hualapai Way, Ste. 130-86
Las Vegas, NV 89166 U.S.A
HistriaBooks.com

Gaudium Publishing is an imprint of Histria Books. Titles published under the imprints of Histria Books are distributed worldwide.

All rights reserved. No part of this book may be reprinted or reproduced or utilized in any form or by any electronic, mechanical, or other means, now known or hereafter invented, including photocopying and recording, or in any information storage or retrieval system, without the permission in writing from the Publisher.

Library of Congress Control Number: 2023938033

ISBN: 978-1-59211-311-8 (casebound)
ISBN: 978-1-59211-321-7 (eBook)

Copyright ©2023 by Alicia Shevetone

dedication

TO FATIMA,
WHO FUNDAMENTALLY
ALTERED THE TRAJECTORY
OF MY LIFE
WITH ONE FATEFUL
INTRODUCTION.

APPETIZERS 11

Baked Brie with Rum Chutney	12
Fried Picklebacks	15
Chicken Marsala Meatballs	16
Salmon Pinwheels	19
Dirty Flatbreads	20
G&T Cucumber Sandwiches	23
Martini Dip	24
Duck Pâté	27
Swiss Fondue	28
Cheesy Bourbon Bites	31

SOUPS 33

Sopa de Pipián Verde	35
Gazpacho and Bloody Mary Granita	36
Crab Chowder	39
Split Pea Soup	40
Borscht	43
Bouillabaisse with Rouille	44
Whiskey Potato Soup	47
Albondigas with Fiesta Crema	48
Cream of Mushroom Soup	51
Cod & Red Miso Soup	52

ENTREES 55

Whiskey Short Ribs	57
Portobello Fajitas	58
Lasagna Alla Vodka	61
Mussels with Vermouth	62
Gin-ger Scampi	65
Manhattan Ribs	66
Lamb Chops with Mojito Chimichurri	69
Creamy Peppercorn Patties	70
Orange Chicken	73
Beef Stroganoff	74

SIDES 77

Mac & 'Due	79
Sloppy Peas	80
Spinach Rockefeller	83
French Onion Crostata	84
Cranberry Sauce	87
Lentilles Françaises	88
Fennel Cutlets and Orange Dipping Sauce	91
Maple Bourbon Sweet Potatoes	92
Mushrooms Borrachos	95
Risotto Inverno	96

DESSERTS 99

Currant Challah Pudding with Crème AngLazy	101
Amaretti	102
Chocolate Hazelnut "Mousse"	105
Blackberry Clafoutis	106
Piña Colada Panna Cotta	109
Russian Shake	110
Limoncello Trifle	113
Cannoli Tiramisu	114
Mudslide Pie	117
Subayune	118

WITH A TITLE LIKE *FOOD WITH SPIRIT*, YOU MIGHT BE THINKING, "I BET THIS GIRL LOVES TO DRINK."

INTRODUCTION

GUILTY, but if it's not cabernet, vodka, or rum, I tap out pretty quickly. My grandparents owned two bars and a restaurant in San Jose, California, where I was born and raised. Some of my earliest memories were in those bars, propped up next to the registers, with my grandmother counting cash.

I met my husband, Mark, at a bar. (I later learned it was a set-up by my friend, Fatima, who was desperately trying to inject some fun into my then-dismal existence as a law student and full-time banker.) Mark's family was also in the bar business in San Jose, long before we met. Incidentally, Mark has very little interest in spirits outside of an occasional snifter of well-aged Scotch or a shot of high-end tequila.

Then how is it that a cookbook author, pondering the theme of her third cookbook, lands on such an unlikely subject as food with spirit? Turns out, my fascination with alcohol-laced delights dates back quite a ways.

Decades before "boozy brunches" were a thing, my family had a talent for infusing food with spirits. My mom, the gourmet against whom I measure all others, used to make the most—the most—delectable chocolate bourbon balls. When I was a kid, it was not uncommon for me to inhale a dozen before holiday company arrived, even though I had no idea what bourbon was. As the years went on, I developed an even deeper appreciation for cuisine that blurs the lines between food and spirits. The recipes in this cookbook range from bold and unexpected mashups like my Dirty Flatbreads, to elegant creations like my Spinach Rockefeller. No matter your culinary skill level, my hope is that you'll have as much fun trying these recipes as I had writing—and testing—them!

CHEERS!

appetizers

SAVORY MORSELS

that fulfill their destiny in one or two bites—precious appetizers, how I adore thee! My anecdotal research reveals that it is nearly impossible to be glum when in the presence of appetizers. Hand-held, mobile, and festive, appetizers are the quintessential party food.

I spent the better part of 2021 developing appetizer recipes. In fact, my first live television appearance was an appetizer demonstration of my Grape & Mortadella Crostini, one of the stand-out favorites from my first cookbook, *Italian Cookbook for Two*. Soon after, my appetizer obsession ignited a series of sold-out pop-ups in Las Vegas, which I lovingly branded as my Appy Hours.

This chapter features ten of my favorite liquor-infused hors d'oeuvres. Some are intensely boozy, others are elegantly subtle, and all should spark some very colorful banter at your next cocktail party.

SALUTI!

baked brie WITH RUM CHUTNEY

Prediction: This chutney will ignite your creativity in ways you've yet to even imagine! Instead of brie, slather it on roast pork. Smear it on toast. Swirl it into your yogurt. Who are we kidding? You need the brie.

SERVES: 4 | PREP TIME: 5 MIN | COOK TIME: 1 HR + 15 MIN | TOTAL TIME: 1 HR + 20 MIN

3 cups frozen cherries, thawed and patted dry

1/4 cup minced shallot

1 1/2 cups packed light brown sugar

3/4 cup apple cider vinegar

1/4 cup spiced rum

One 8-ounce wheel of brie

Sprigs of rosemary, for garnish

Sliced baguette and crudités, for serving

To prepare the chutney, combine cherries, shallot, brown sugar, and apple cider vinegar in a small pot over medium heat until boiling.

Reduce heat to medium low; add rum.

Cook, uncovered, for 1 hour.

Preheat the oven to 350F.

Slice the rind off the top of the brie and place the brie in the center of an ovenproof baking dish. Bake for 10–15 minutes, until warm and slightly melted.

Remove brie from the oven and surround it with the rum chutney. Garnish with sprigs of rosemary and serve with sliced baguette and crudités.

fried PICKLEBACKS

For the uninitiated, a pickleback is a shot of whiskey followed by a pickle juice chaser. It's one of those unexpected combinations that can only be improved when fried. I use "hamburger dill chips" for this because they are bite-sized and perfectly poppable. Bet you can't eat just one!

SERVES: 4 | PREP TIME: 10 MIN | COOK TIME: 60 MIN | TOTAL TIME: 1 HR + 10 MIN

FOR THE WHISKEY DIPPING SAUCE

- 1/2 cup mayonnaise
- 1/4 creamy horseradish
- 2 tablespoons ketchup
- 1 teaspoon whiskey

FOR THE FRIED PICKLEBACKS

- 2 cups vegetable oil
- 2 cups all-purpose flour
- 1/4 cup cornstarch
- 2 teaspoons kosher salt
- 1 teaspoon ground black pepper
- 1 teaspoon garlic powder
- 1 teaspoon onion powder
- 1 egg
- 3/4 cup buttermilk
- 1/4 cup whiskey
- 16 ounces dill pickle chips, drained and patted dry

MAKE THE WHISKEY DIPPING SAUCE

Combine all ingredients and chill until serving.

MAKE THE FRIED PICKLEBACKS

Heat the vegetable oil to 375F in a deep, large skillet.

In a shallow bowl, combine flour, cornstarch, salt, pepper, garlic powder, and onion powder. In a second shallow bowl, whisk the egg and add buttermilk and whiskey to combine.

Place one quarter of the pickle slices in the buttermilk mixture and toss to coat. Using a slotted spoon, lift the pickles and let any excess batter drain back into the bowl. Place the batter coated pickles in the flour mixture and toss to coat evenly.

Shake off any excess flour mixture and add the pickles to the hot oil, ensuring they don't clump together. Fry pickles until crispy and golden, about 2 minutes. Using a clean slotted spoon or a spider, transfer the pickles to a cooling rack.

If desired, sprinkle fried pickles with additional salt. Repeat with the remaining three batches of pickles.

Serve immediately with whiskey dipping sauce.

chicken marsala MEATBALLS

Chicken Marsala is traditionally prepared with thin slices of chicken breast, called scaloppini, enveloped in a luscious brown gravy made with a buttery reduction of Sicilian fortified wine. Transformed into juicy chicken meatballs, this saucy reboot is sure to replace Swedish Meatballs as the new party favorite.

SERVES: 4 | PREP TIME: 15 MIN | COOK TIME: 25 MIN | TOTAL TIME: 40 MIN

FOR THE MEATBALLS

- 1 pound ground chicken (50/50 dark/white blend is best)
- 1/2 cup freshly grated Parmesan
- 1/4 cup chopped fresh Italian parsley
- 2 tablespoons whole milk
- 1/2 teaspoon salt
- 1 teaspoon Italian seasoning
- 1/4 cup breadcrumbs
- 1 large egg, beaten
- 1/2 cup all-purpose flour
- 2 tablespoons olive oil

MAKE THE MEATBALLS

In a large bowl, add Parmesan, parsley, milk, salt, Italian seasoning, breadcrumbs, and egg and stir to combine. Add the chicken and gently combine. Shape into one-inch balls. Dust each meatball in the flour.

Add 2 tablespoons of olive oil to a large skillet over medium heat. Add half of the meatballs to the pan, making sure not to overcrowd them. Sauté the meatballs until cooked through, about 3-4 minutes. Transfer cooked meatballs to a plate and season with a pinch of salt.

Repeat to cook the remaining meatballs.

FOR THE MARSALA SAUCE

- 1 tablespoon olive oil
- 1/2 cup sliced shallots 1/4" thick
- 2 teaspoons minced garlic
- 4 ounces sliced mushrooms
- 1/2 teaspoon salt
- 1/2 cup sweet Marsala
- 2 tablespoons chopped fresh thyme
- 1/2 cup low-sodium chicken broth
- 1 tablespoon chopped parsley, for garnish

MAKE THE MARSALA SAUCE

Add 1 tablespoon of oil to the same skillet. Add the shallot and garlic and cook until fragrant, about 30 seconds. Add the mushrooms to the pan and sauté, stirring frequently until tender, about 5 minutes. Add a little more olive oil if the pan is dry. Season the mushrooms with 1/2 teaspoon salt. Deglaze the pan with the Marsala, increase heat to high, and loosen anything that is sticking to the bottom of the pan. Simmer the sauce until the Marsala reduces by half, about 5 minutes. Add broth and thyme, reduce the heat to medium, and simmer until the sauce reduces by half, about 5 minutes.

PUT IT TOGETHER:

Add chicken meatballs and any juices that collected on the plate back into the pan. Coat the meatballs in the sauce and simmer until the meatballs are warmed through, 2-3 minutes. Garnish with chopped parsley.

salmon PINWHEELS

Hosting brunch? This keto-friendly appetizer is the perfect way to welcome your guests. Everything you love about bagels, without the heavy carbs. And where is the booze hidden? In the cream cheese—purely to make it spreadable, of course!

SERVES: 4 | PREP TIME: 15 MIN | INACTIVE: 3 HRS | TOTAL TIME: 3 HRS + 15 MIN

1 cucumber

8 ounces smoked salmon

1/2 cup cream cheese

1/4 teaspoon black pepper

1 tablespoon chopped dill

1 tablespoon vodka

1 tablespoon capers, rinsed and patted dry

2 tablespoons shaved red onion

2 tablespoons everything bagel seasoning

Using a vegetable peeler, peel thin strips of cucumber lengthwise, making sure to stop just as the cucumber seeds become visible. On a clean, flat surface, shingle the strips of cucumber lengthwise, overlapping the edge slightly.

Top the cucumber with a layer of salmon.

Combine cream cheese, pepper, dill, and vodka.

Spread the cream cheese mixture over the salmon and sprinkle with capers and red onion.

Carefully lift the bottom of the cucumber slices and roll to the top, creating a long cylinder. Wrap the cylinder in plastic wrap and freeze for 2-3 hours until firm.

Using a serrated knife, slice pinwheels about an inch wide.

Sprinkle the pinwheels with everything bagel seasoning and serve.

dirty FLATBREADS

Dirty Martini meets Flatbread, falls in love, and honeymoons in your tummy! Consider the ingredients in this tapenade recipe to be a loose guide that you can adapt to your palate. Capers, dill relish, pimentos... As long as there's vodka and olives, you're good.

SERVES: 4 | PREP TIME: 15 MIN | COOK TIME: 10 MIN | TOTAL TIME: 25 MIN

FOR THE TAPENADE

- 1 cup green olives
- 1 teaspoon anchovy paste (or 1 chopped anchovy)
- 1/2 teaspoon salt
- 1/2 teaspoon minced garlic
- 2 tablespoons chopped chives
- 2 tablespoons chopped parsley
- 1/4 cup extra virgin olive oil
- 1 teaspoon lemon zest
- 1 teaspoon lemon juice
- 2 tablespoons vodka

FOR THE FLATBREADS

- 4 naan flatbreads (about 4 ounces each)
- 1/2 cup onion jam
- 1/2 cup blue cheese crumbles

MAKE THE TAPENADE

Add all ingredients to a food processor and pulse until the mixture is coarsely blended.

MAKE THE FLATBREADS

Prepare the naan according to package directions.

Spread 2 tablespoons of onion jam over each warm naan. Top the onion jam with a layer of tapenade, about 2 tablespoons. Sprinkle two tablespoons of blue cheese crumbles over the top.

Serve immediately.

g+t CUCUMBER SANDWICHES

My favorite Brit, a gin-lover to her core, taught me that all proper English sandwiches boast a smear of butter on the inside. These smashing sandwiches are cheeky enough to make you smile, but not boozy enough to get you pissed.

SERVES: 4 | PREP TIME: 10 MIN | INACTIVE: 15 MIN | TOTAL TIME: 25 MIN

2 teaspoons gin

1/4 cup tonic

1/2 English cucumber, sliced 1/8-inch thick

1 teaspoon black pepper

1 teaspoon salt

8 slices soft white sandwich bread (about 1/2 a loaf), crusts removed

8 ounces cream cheese, softened

1 tablespoon lemon juice

1/4 teaspoon garlic powder

4 tablespoons butter, softened

2 tablespoons chopped fresh dill

In a bowl, combine gin, tonic, pepper, and salt.

Add cucumber slices and refrigerate for 15 minutes. Drain the cucumber slices and pat dry with clean paper towels.

Combine cream cheese, lemon juice, and garlic powder; set aside.

Spread one side of each slice of bread with a thin layer of butter, followed by a layer of the cream cheese mixture.

Shingle 1/4 of the cucumber slices over 4 of the bread slices. Top with remaining bread slices to complete 4 sandwiches.

Cut each sandwich into quarters, yielding 16 sandwiches.

martini DIP

Admit it. Right now, you are wondering why you didn't think of this. A dip that is made entirely of your favorite gin martini, cream cheese, and sour cream? Make it a double.

SERVES: 4 | PREP TIME: 10 MIN | TOTAL TIME: 10 MIN

10 green olives

1/4 cup pimentos, drained

1-2 teaspoons gin, to taste

1 cup cream cheese

1/4 cup sour cream

1/2 teaspoon salt (optional, depending on the olives you use)

Pulse in a food processor until smooth.

Serve with mini peppers, celery sticks, and crackers.

duck PÂTÉ

French for paste, pâté is the quintessential seasoned schmear for toasted baguette. This version is inspired by the recipe of legendary chef Jacques Pépin, whose ability to distill often-intimidating French cuisine down to its bare essence is très magnifique. Bon appétit!

SERVES: 4 | PREP TIME: 5 MIN | COOK: 10 MIN | INACTIVE: 2 HRS
TOTAL TIME: 2 HRS + 15 MIN

- 3 ounces duck fat
- 2 tablespoons shallot
- 3 ounces duck liver, cut into 1-inch pieces
- 1/4 teaspoon Italian seasoning
- 1/8 teaspoon dried tarragon
- 1 teaspoon chopped garlic
- 1/4 teaspoon salt
- 1/4 teaspoon freshly ground black pepper
- 1 teaspoon Cognac
- 16 slices of toasted baguette, about 1/4-inch thick

In a small pan over medium high heat, melt duck fat in a skillet and allow it to slightly brown, about 4-5 minutes. Add the shallots and sauté until fragrant, about 30 seconds. Add the liver, Italian seasoning, tarragon, garlic, salt, and pepper and cook for 2 minutes.

Transfer the mixture to a food processor, add the Cognac, and blend until smooth.

Cool the mixture for 2 hours at room temperature, then refrigerate until serving.

Spread the pâté on the toasted baguette slices, and serve.

Swiss Fondue

Emmental is a fancy word for Swiss cheese—but this isn't the time for the pre-sliced, holey stuff. Amazing fondue requires a combination of freshly grated Emmental and Gruyère, flavored with a clear, cherry brandy called Kirschwasser (kirsch, for short). Don't have kirsch on hand? Substitute vermouth or bourbon.

SERVES: 6 | PREP TIME: 10 MIN | COOK TIME: 20 MIN | TOTAL TIME: 30 MIN

1/2 garlic clove

3/4 cups dry white wine

3/4 cup chicken stock

2 cups grated Emmental

2 cups grated Gruyère

1 tablespoon cornstarch

2 teaspoons kirsch

4 cups cubed baguette

Rub the inside of a fondue pot with the cut side of the garlic clove, then discard it. Add wine and stock to the pot over moderate heat, until simmering.

Gradually add both cheeses to the pot and cook, stirring constantly in a zigzag pattern until cheese is completely melted. Reduce the heat to ensure that it isn't boiling.

In a small bowl, combine cornstarch and kirsch to form a slurry, and slowly add it to the fondue, stirring constantly.

Continue to cook and stir the fondue until thickened, about 5 minutes.

Serve with cubed baguette.

cheesy bourbon BITES

Taleggio is a velvety, semi-soft Italian cheese—and it's the next big thing. Perfectly meltable, it pairs beautifully with fig preserves and bourbon. You can easily find mini pastry shells, phyllo cups, and other premade tartlets online or in stores. In a pinch, substitute canned crescent rolls or biscuit dough, press into a mini muffin tin, and bake according to package directions.

SERVES: 4 | PREP TIME: 10 MIN | COOK TIME: 10 MIN | TOTAL TIME: 20 MIN

- 1/4 cup walnuts, chopped
- 1/3 cup fig preserves
- 1 tablespoon bourbon
- 8 ounces Taleggio cheese (or substitute brie)
- 16 mini pastry shells

To toast the walnuts, place them in a small skillet over medium heat for 3 minutes. Stir often and watch closely to avoid burning.

Preheat the oven to 350F.

Add fig preserves and bourbon in a small bowl and stir to combine.

Remove the rind from the Taleggio, discard the rind, then cut the Taleggio into cubes, about 1/4-inch square.

Place the pastry shells on a sheet pan. Place a cube of Taleggio into each shell and top with 1/2 teaspoon of the fig mixture. Top with toasted walnuts.

Bake for 10 minutes, or until the Taleggio is bubbling and melted.

Remove from the oven and serve warm.

Soups

IS THERE ANYTHING MORE COMFORTING THAN A BOWL OF SOUP?

Yes, a bowl of soup with an attitude!! Each soup in this chapter has an edgy twist that is sure to satisfy and inspire. But you're in for more than just intense flavor.

You'll learn how to:
- use pumpkin seeds as an ultra-cool vegan thickener
- transform sour cream into a party condiment
- fold aluminum foil into the ultimate fish packets

Whether you're vegetarian, pescatarian, or boozetarian, grab your spoon and commence salivation!

KANPAI!

sopa DE PIPIÁN VERDE

Inspired by the classic green mole, this vegetarian soup is thickened with pumpkin seeds to achieve a subtle complexity. Mezcal adds warmth and earthiness, an unexpected balance with the vibrant green chiles.

SERVES: 2 | PREP TIME: 10 MIN | COOK TIME: 25 MIN | TOTAL TIME: 35 MIN

1 tablespoon olive oil

1/4 cup diced onion

1/4 teaspoon salt

1 teaspoon sweet paprika

1 teaspoon ground cumin

1/2 teaspoon dried oregano

2 tablespoons mezcal

2 cups vegetable broth

8 ounces canned diced green chiles

4 tablespoons shelled pumpkin seeds

2 tablespoons chopped cilantro

1 diced avocado

Warm olive oil in a stockpot over medium heat. Add the onion and salt and sauté for 5 minutes. Stir in the spices and jalapeno and cook and additional 2 minutes.

Deglaze with mezcal, loosening any vegetables that are sticking to the bottom of the pot, about 1 minute. Add vegetable broth and diced green chiles. Bring to a boil, then reduce to a simmer.

In a blender, add pumpkin seeds and 1/2 cup of water. Purée until smooth.

Add puréed pumpkin seeds to simmering stew and stir occasionally, 10-15 minutes.

Remove stew from the heat, stir in the lime juice and season to taste with salt and pepper.

Garnish with cilantro and avocado.

gazpacho AND BLOODY MARY GRANITA

Having a refreshing cold soup in your repertoire for steamy days is a godsend; but who are we kidding? Gazpacho's primary role here is to serve as a savory pillow for the icy, spicy granita.

SERVES: 6 | PREP TIME: 20 MIN | INACTIVE: 12 HRS | TOTAL TIME: 12 HRS + 20 MIN

FOR THE BLOODY MARY GRANITA

- 6 ounces vine-ripened tomatoes, quartered and seeded
- 1 tablespoons water
- 1 tablespoons vodka
- 1/2 teaspoon Worcestershire sauce
- 1/2 teaspoon lemon juice
- 1/4 teaspoon smoked paprika
- 2 dashes hot sauce
- 1/2 teaspoon salt

MAKE THE BLOODY MARY GRANITA

Add the tomatoes, water, vodka, Worcestershire, lemon juice, paprika, hot sauce, and salt to a blender and blend on high for 1 minute. Pour into a loaf pan or glass dish.

Freeze for 2 hours, then use a fork to scrape the mixture and distribute the icy crystals back into an even layer. Return to the freezer until completely frozen, about 2 more hours.

FOR THE GAZPACHO

- 2 pounds vine-ripened tomatoes, quartered and seeded
- 8 ounces roughly chopped seedless cucumber, peeled
- 3 ounces green bell pepper, cored, seeded, and roughly chopped
- 1/2 cup roughly chopped red onion
- 1 slice white bread, crusts removed, moistened with water
- 1 teaspoon chopped garlic
- 2 tablespoons apple cider vinegar
- 1 teaspoon salt
- 3 tablespoons extra virgin olive oil
- 1/2 teaspoon black pepper
- Celery salt, to sprinkle

MAKE THE GAZPACHO

Combine tomatoes, cucumber, bell pepper, onion, bread, garlic, vinegar, and salt in a blender and blend at high speed until completely smooth, 1-2 minutes.

Lower the blender speed to medium and slowly drizzle in the olive oil. Continue to blend until gazpacho is emulsified and creamy.

Refrigerate for 4 hours.

Serve in bowls. Use a fork to scrape the desired amount of bloody mary granita to garnish the gazpacho, followed by a sprinkle of celery salt.

crab CHOWDER

It's time to get real. The only reason this recipe exists is because when I learned how many steps are involved in making a crab bisque, I rolled my eyes and decided to make a crabby version of my Mom's clam chowder. If you're short on time, omit the potatoes, and simmer it a little longer to thicken.

SERVES: 4 | PREP TIME: 20 MIN | COOK TIME: 35 MIN | TOTAL TIME: 55 MIN

4 ounces potatoes, peeled and cubed

1 1/2 teaspoons salt

1 teaspoon onion powder

1 teaspoon garlic powder

1/2 cup minced onion

1/2 cup minced celery

1/4 cup butter

1/4 cup all-purpose flour

3 cups seafood broth, fish stock, or clam juice

1 teaspoon chopped fresh thyme

2 cups half-and-half

12 ounces lump crab meat

1 teaspoon white pepper

3 tablespoons sherry

2 tablespoons chopped parsley

Place potatoes in a small pot. Cover with about an inch of cold water and add 1 teaspoon salt, onion powder, and garlic powder. Boil until al dente, about 15 minutes. Drain potatoes and set aside.

In a large soup pot, melt the butter over medium heat. Once the butter begins to foam, sauté the onion and celery until tender, about 3 minutes. Sprinkle the flour over the onions and cook for 1 minute.

Gradually add the seafood broth (or stock or clam juice), stirring constantly, until well combined.

Add cooked potatoes, remaining 1/2 teaspoon salt, thyme, and half-and-half, and increase heat to high. Bring to a boil, stirring frequently. Reduce to medium low and simmer for 5 minutes.

Add crab, white pepper, and sherry, reduce heat to low, and cook an additional 5 minutes.

To serve, divide chowder into 4 bowls and garnish with chopped parsley.

split pea SOUP

Thick, meaty, inviting... This soup is as hearty as it is elegant. The sherry is subtle, while the nutmeg adds an unmistakable warmth. A big green sweater in a bowl.

SERVES: 6 | PREP TIME: 15 MIN | COOK TIME: 2 HRS + 10 MIN | TOTAL TIME: 2 HRS + 25 M

3 tablespoons butter

1 1/2 cups diced onion

1 cup diced celery

1/2 cup diced carrots

1 teaspoon minced garlic

5 cups low-sodium chicken stock

3 cups filtered water

16 ounces dried split peas, picked over and rinsed

2 bay leaves

1 tablespoon chopped fresh thyme

2 teaspoons black pepper

2 teaspoons salt

1 ham bone or ham hock

12 ounces diced ham steak

2 tablespoons dry sherry

1/4 teaspoon freshly grated nutmeg

Heat butter in a large pot over medium-high heat. Once melted, add onion, celery, and carrots and sauté until softened, about 3 minutes. Add garlic and sauté until fragrant, about 30 seconds.

Add chicken stock, water, split peas, bay leaves, and thyme. Season with pepper and 1 teaspoon of salt. Nestle ham bone/hock into soup mixture.

Increase heat to high and bring mixture to a boil. Reduce heat to low, cover and simmer, for 60 minutes, stirring occasionally.

Discard ham bone/hock, add the diced ham, cover the soup and simmer, stirring occasionally, until peas are completely tender, about another hour.

Use a potato masher to press the peas until they completely disintegrate.

Taste and add remaining 1 teaspoon of salt, if needed.

Before serving, stir in sherry and nutmeg.

borscht

This classic Russian beet soup is just the thing to dazzle your guests. Its crimson color and hearty flavors are the perfect base for an elegant swirl of sour cream and dill. And if you thin out your sour cream with vodka instead of half-and-half, I won't tell a soul.

SERVES: 4 | PREP TIME: 10 MIN | COOK TIME: 1HR + 15 MIN | TOTAL TIME: 1 HR + 25 MIN

3 tablespoons olive oil

1 cup diced onion

3 teaspoons minced garlic

1/2 cup diced celery

1 cup diced carrots

2 cups diced beets

2 cups chopped red cabbage

2 tablespoons tomato paste

1 teaspoon celery seed

1/2 teaspoon allspice

2 tablespoons vodka

6 cups beef stock

2 teaspoons salt

1 teaspoon pepper

1/4 cup sour cream

2 tablespoons half-and-half

Add olive oil to a large pot over medium heat. Once oil is shimmering, add onions and garlic and sauté until softened, about 5 minutes. Add celery, carrots, beets, and cabbage and cook an additional 5 minutes.

Scoot some of the veggies to the side and toast the tomato paste, celery seed, and allspice for about 30 seconds, until fragrant.

Deglaze with vodka for 1-2 minutes and scrape the bottom of the pot to release any vegetables that are sticking. Add the stock, salt, and pepper and increase heat to high. Bring to a boil, then reduce heat to medium low. Simmer until the vegetables are completely tender, at least an hour.

Season with additional salt and pepper, as needed. Allow the soup to cool, then purée until smooth.

Combine sour cream and half-and-half. Drizzle over the soup.

bouillabaisse

A seafood-forward, Provençal soup, featuring anise-flavored liqueur, accompanied by mayo-slathered, toasted bread? Oui, bien sûr! Grandma Barbara, this one is for you. And our homies back in Marseille.

SERVES: 4 | PREP TIME: 20 MIN | COOK TIME: 25 MIN | TOTAL TIME: 45 MIN

FOR THE ROUILLE
- 1 cup mayonnaise
- 1 tablespoon chopped garlic
- 1/2 red bell pepper, roasted, peeled, and seeded
- 1/4 teaspoon black pepper
- Pinch of saffron

MAKE THE ROUILLE
Combine all ingredients in a food processor and purée until smooth.

Refrigerate until serving.

FOR THE SOUP
- 3 tablespoons olive oil
- 1/2 cup diced leek, white and pale-green parts only
- 3/4 cup diced fennel, fronds reserved
- 1/2 cup diced celery
- 1/2 cup diced carrots
- 1/2 teaspoon salt
- 1/2 teaspoon ground pepper
- 2 teaspoons minced garlic
- 1 1/2 cups fresh, peeled, diced tomatoes
- 1 bay leaf
- 1 orange peel (about 2 inches long)
- 1/2 teaspoon saffron
- 1 teaspoon chopped fresh thyme
- 3 3/4 cups seafood stock or clam juice
- 1/4 cup anise-flavored liqueur
- 8 ounces cod, cut into 2-inch pieces
- 8 ounces lobster, cut into 2-inch pieces
- 12 jumbo shrimp (21/25 per pound), peeled and deveined
- 12 mussels, cleaned and de-bearded
- 12 crostini

MAKE THE SOUP

Add the olive oil to a large pot over medium-high heat. When hot, add leeks, diced fennel, celery, and carrot and sauté until softened, about 5 minutes. Season vegetables with salt and pepper. Add garlic, tomatoes, bay leaf, orange peel, saffron, and thyme and cook for another 5 minutes, stirring frequently.

Add seafood stock and liqueur. Once boiling, reduce heat to medium-low, add cod and lobster, and simmer for 2 minutes. Add shrimp and mussels and simmer until mussels open and shrimp is pink and cooked through, about 5 minutes.

Discard the bay leaf, orange peel, and any mussels that don't open.

For serving, divide the soup evenly, and place 3 mussels and 3 shrimp in each bowl. Spread a thin layer of rouille on each crostino and garnish each bowl with 3 crostini and a few fennel fronds.

Serve extra rouille on the side to stir into the soup, if desired.

whiskey potato SOUP

This soup tastes like a stuffed baked potato with a sidecar of sass! Scallions and bacon can easily be replaced with a few broccoli florets, a dollop of sour cream, or even crushed potato chips.

SERVES: 4 | PREP TIME: 15 MIN | COOK TIME: 35 MIN | TOTAL TIME: 50 MIN

2 tablespoons butter

2 teaspoons minced garlic

1 cup diced onion

1/4 cup whiskey

3 cups peeled and diced potatoes

4 cups chicken stock

1 1/2 teaspoons salt

1/2 cup half-and-half

10 ounces shredded cheddar cheese

1/2 teaspoon pepper

1/4 cup diced scallions

1 cup chopped bacon

Melt the butter in a large pot over medium heat. Once the butter begins to foam, add garlic and onions and sauté until softened, about 3 minutes. Reduce heat to low and add the whiskey. Simmer for 3 minutes.

Increase heat to medium, add the potatoes, stock, and salt to the pot and simmer until the potatoes are completely cooked, about 25 minutes. Stir in the half-and-half and, once simmering, turn off the heat.

Using an immersion blender, purée until smooth.

Add the cheddar and stir to combine, returning soup to low heat, if needed, until completely melted. Season with pepper, thinning with additional chicken stock, if desired.

Garnish with scallions and bacon.

albóndigas WITH FIESTA CREMA

This creative spin on Albóndigas features delightful Mexican meatballs fortified with crushed corn chips, floating in a blissful beefy broth flavored with distinctive notes of cumin and oregano. Paired with a boozy crema, this soup is a party in a bowl!

SERVES: 8 | PREP TIME: 10 MIN | INACTIVE TIME: 30 MIN | COOK TIME: 30 MIN
TOTAL TIME: 1 HR + 10 MIN

FOR THE FIESTA CREMA
- 1 teaspoon lime juice
- 1/4 teaspoon ground cumin
- 2 teaspoons pico de gallo
- 1/4 cup Mexican crema
- 1/2 teaspoon tequila blanco

MAKE THE THE FIESTA CREMA
Combine all ingredients and refrigerate until serving.

FOR THE ALBÓNDIGAS
- 1 pound lean ground beef
- 4 eggs, beaten
- 1 cup diced red onion
- 1/2 cup crushed corn chips
- 1/4 cup chopped cilantro
- 2 teaspoons salt
- 1 teaspoon red pepper flakes
- 1 tablespoon dried oregano
- 1 teaspoon ground cumin
- 6 cups chicken stock
- 1 14.5 ounce can diced tomatoes
- 1 cup chopped carrots
- 1/2 cup chopped celery
- 1 bay leaf

MAKE THE THE ALBÓNDIGAS

In a medium bowl, combine beef, eggs, 1/2 cup onion, chips, cilantro, 1 teaspoon salt, red pepper flakes, oregano, and cumin. Refrigerate mixture for 30 minutes.

In a large pot over high heat, add stock, tomatoes with their juice, carrots, celery, remaining 1/2 cup onion, remaining teaspoon of salt, and bay leaf. Once the broth begins to boil; reduce heat to low.

Remove the beef mixture from the refrigerator and form into meatballs, about an inch in diameter. Add the meatballs to the soup and cover the pot.

Cook for 20 minutes, until vegetables are tender and meatballs are cooked through.

Discard the bay leaf. Serve with a dollop of Fiesta Crema.

cream of mushroom SOUP

One of the Top 10 Most Wanted Soups, Cream of Mushroom has a rap sheet a dozen ingredients long. Turns out vermouth and mushrooms are the Bonnie and Clyde of the rowdy soup crowd. Earthy, sassy, and dangerous, it's quite possible that you'll never think of them separately again.

SERVES: 6 | PREP TIME: 10 MIN | COOK TIME: 1 HR + 5 MIN | TOTAL TIME: 1 HR + 15 MIN

1/4 cup extra virgin olive oil

1/4 cup butter

2 pounds chopped cremini mushrooms

1/2 cup minced shallots

2 tablespoons all-purpose flour

2 tablespoons dry vermouth

1 teaspoon white pepper

4 cups half-and-half

1 cup chicken stock

1 teaspoon salt, optional

2 tablespoons chopped chives

2 tablespoons chopped parsley

In a large pot over medium heat, add the olive oil and butter. Once butter is melted and begins to foam, increase heat to medium high, add mushrooms and shallots, and sauté until the vegetables cook down to a paste, about 30 minutes.

Add flour and stir the mushrooms.

Add vermouth and deglaze, loosening any vegetables and flour that may be sticking to the bottom of the pan. Reduce heat to medium low.

Add white pepper, half-and-half, and chicken stock and simmer, uncovered, for 30 minutes, stirring occasionally.

Using an immersion blender, purée the soup in the pot until smooth.

Season with salt, if needed, and serve topped with chopped chives and chopped parsley.

cod & red miso SOUP

You might think that the sexy red miso in this recipe steals the show, until you get to the cod in its ultra-chic aluminum foil sake packet. Red miso gets top billing, but the cod goes home with the award.

SERVES: 4 | PREP TIME: 15 MIN | COOK TIME: 40 MIN | TOTAL TIME: 55 MIN

FOR THE DASHI

- 8 cups mushroom broth
- 1 4"x4" piece kombu (dried kelp)

MAKE THE THE DASHI

Add mushroom broth and kombu to a large pot over high heat. When the broth begins to boil, reduce heat to medium and simmer for 15 minutes.

Discard the kombu.

FOR THE FISH

- 4 4-ounce cod filets
- 1/2 cup sake
- 1/2 cup dashi
- 1 teaspoon salt
- 1 teaspoon pepper
- 2 teaspoons minced ginger
- 2 teaspoons minced garlic

MAKE THE THE FISH

Preheat oven to 425F.

In a medium bowl, add sake, 1/2 cup of dashi, salt, pepper, ginger, and garlic; stir to combine. Coat each piece of cod in the mixture.

Lay out four sheets of aluminum foil (about 12"x12" each). Place one cod filet on each sheet of foil. Loosely fold up the sides of each sheet of foil to form a bowl shape, then pour 1/4 of the sake mixture over each filet. Fold the foil over each filet to seal, creating four enclosed foil packets.

Set the packets on a baking sheet and bake until cooked through, about 15-20 minutes depending on thickness.

Once cooked, carefully open each foil packet to release the steam; prepare the dashi.

FOR THE SOUP

1/4 cup red miso paste

7 1/2 cups dashi

1/2 cup diced scallions

Sesame seeds, for garnish

MAKE THE THE SOUP

Gently simmer the dashi over medium heat.

Place the miso in a fine sieve and lower the bottom of the sieve into the simmering dashi. Using the back of a spoon, gently press the miso through the sieve into the dashi. Stir dashi well to incorporate the miso.

Transfer each cooked cod filet to a bowl. Pour an equal amount of soup in each bowl.

Garnish with scallions and sesame seeds.

entrées

ENTRÉES MEAN BIGGER PORTIONS, WHICH MEANS MORE ALCOHOL.
You're in for a couple of meat-free options, some shellfish dishes, some spectacular reboots to old favorites, and some stick-to-your-ribs… well, ribs!

The recipes in this chapter are as diverse as they are savory. From gin to mezcal, I hope the flavor combinations will both inspire and delight. If you really want to wow your friends, make a specialty cocktail featuring the spirit found in the recipe: maybe a mezcal mule with the fajitas or extra Manhattans to go with the ribs.

SKÅL!

whiskey SHORT RIBS

Stewed meat prepared in a multicooker is a weeknight lifesaver. Add whiskey to the braising liquid, and you have an instant classic.

**SERVES: 4 | PREP TIME: 15 MIN | COOK TIME: 1 HR + 5 MIN | INACTIVE TIME: 15 MIN
TOTAL TIME: 1 HR + 35 MIN**

- 3 tablespoons extra virgin olive oil
- 4 boneless beef short ribs
- 2 teaspoons salt
- 1/2 teaspoon ground black pepper
- 1/2 cup diced onion
- 1/2 cup diced carrot
- 2 cups shredded cabbage
- 1 teaspoon minced garlic
- 1 tablespoon tomato paste
- 3 tablespoons whiskey
- 3/4 cup beef stock
- 1 teaspoon Worcestershire sauce
- 2 sprigs fresh thyme
- 2 tablespoons butter
- Chopped Italian parsley, for garnish

Turn the multicooker to sauté mode and add 2 tablespoons of olive oil. Pat short ribs dry and season all sides with salt and pepper. Add short ribs to the multicooker and sear all sides until browned (about 10 minutes total). Transfer short ribs to a plate.

Add remaining tablespoon of olive oil, carrots, and onions. Cook for 5 minutes, stirring occasionally. Add cabbage and garlic and cook for 1 minute, stirring frequently. Add tomato paste and cook 2 minutes more, stirring frequently. Add the whiskey and scrape the bottom of the multicooker insert to deglaze. Add the beef stock, Worcestershire sauce, and thyme sprigs. Bring to a boil and turn off the multicooker. Add short ribs back into the multicooker and nestle them with the vegetables and broth. Secure the multicooker lid, select pressure cooking mode and set cooking time for 40 minutes. Once 40 minutes have elapsed, allow pressure to naturally release for 15 minutes; then, quick release remaining pressure.

Carefully remove the multicooker lid, remove the thyme sprigs, and transfer the short ribs to a bowl, leaving the vegetables and sauce in the multicooker.

Switch multicooker back to sauté mode, add the butter, and reduce the cooking liquid for 5-10 minutes, until slightly thickened. Season veggies and cooking liquid, as needed, with additional salt and pepper.

Serve the short ribs with veggies and a drizzle of the cooking liquid. Garnish with parsley.

portobello FAJITAS

This dish is more than a recipe—it's dinner theater. When the mezcal hits the piping hot sheet pan, you're in for a smokin' good time! (General Liability Insurance sold separately.)

SERVES: 4 | PREP TIME: 10 MIN | COOK TIME: 20 MIN | TOTAL TIME: 30 MIN

- **3 Portobello mushrooms, stems and gills removed, sliced in about ½" thick slices**
- **12 ounces fresh peppers (like bell, poblano, or Anaheim), thinly sliced**
- **1 small red onion, thinly sliced**
- **1 tablespoon lime juice**
- **2 tablespoons vegetable oil**
- **3 tablespoons taco seasoning**
- **2 tablespoons mezcal**
- **Flour tortillas**
- **Fresh avocado**
- **Lime wedges**
- **Fresh cilantro**

Preheat oven to 425 degrees.

In a large bowl toss sliced mushrooms, peppers, and onions with oil, lime juice, and taco seasoning. Transfer vegetables to a sheet pan and bake 15 minutes. Remove the sheet pan from the oven and move oven rack to the top position, right under the broiler. Place sheet pan on the top rack and broil until the vegetables begin to char, 3-5 more minutes. Remove the sheet pan from the oven and set it on a towel or heat-safe surface.

Pour the mezcal onto the sheet pan and loosen any bits of vegetables that may be stuck to the tray. Toss well.

Serve with blistered tortillas, fresh avocado, lime, and cilantro.

lasagna ALLA VODKA

Individual servings of lasagna paired with a vodka-infused, creamy sauce. Warning: Side effects may include contentment, occasional giddiness, and mild salivation.

**SERVES: 2 | PREP TIME: 15 MIN | COOK TIME: 30 MIN | INACTIVE TIME: 15 MIN
TOTAL TIME: 1 HR**

FOR THE VODKA SAUCE

1 tablespoon olive oil

1 tablespoon butter

1/2 cup minced onion

1 teaspoon minced garlic

1/3 cup vodka

5 ounces tomato purée

1/2 cup heavy cream

1/4 teaspoon salt

1/2 teaspoon black pepper

FOR THE LASAGNA

18 wonton wrappers

Nonstick cooking spray

8 ounces burrata with truffles

6 large fresh basil leaves

6 tablespoons shredded mozzarella

6 tablespoons grated Parmesan

MAKE THE THE VODKA SAUCE

To make the vodka sauce, add olive oil and butter to a large skillet over medium heat. When butter is melted, add onion and garlic and sauté for 2 minutes. Add vodka, stir, and cook for 3 minutes.

Reduce heat to low and add tomato purée and cream. Stir and simmer for 3 minutes. Season with salt and pepper and set aside.

MAKE THE THE LASAGNA

Preheat oven to 350F.

Press a 3-inch biscuit or cookie cutter into each wonton wrapper to create 18 wonton rounds.

Apply a thin layer of cooking spray to a 6-cup muffin pan. Pour a tablespoon of vodka sauce in the well of each muffin cup, followed by one wonton round. Top each wonton round with 1-2 teaspoons of burrata and 1 basil leaf.

Top with another wonton round, more sauce, and the remaining burrata. Top each muffin cup with remaining wonton rounds, a teaspoon more sauce, a tablespoon of mozzarella, and a tablespoon of Parmesan.

Bake for 20 minutes; then allow to cool in the pan for 10-15 minutes, until each Lasagna alla Vodka easily removes from the pan.

mussels WITH VERMOUTH

Vermouth and dairy team up to create a gentle, savory bath for these noble mollusks. No vermouth? A dry white wine is a perfectly acceptable substitute.

SERVES: 4 | PREP TIME: 10 MIN | COOK TIME: 15 MIN | TOTAL TIME: 25 MIN

2 tablespoons extra-virgin olive oil

2 shallots, minced

4 garlic cloves, minced

2 pounds mussels, cleaned

1 cup dry vermouth

1/2 cup heavy cream

4 tablespoons butter

2 tablespoons chopped parsley

1 tablespoon salt

Heat the olive oil in a large pot over medium heat. Sauté shallots and garlic for about 3 minutes. Increase heat to medium high and add the mussels, vermouth, cream, butter, parsley, and salt. Give it a good stir, cover the pot, and cook until mussels open and are cooked through, about 10 minutes.

Divide the mussels and the juices between 2 bowls.

gin-ger SCAMPI

If you love sautéed shrimp, but not the garlicky flavor of scampi, this is the preparation you've been waiting for. Gin and ginger. Clever, right?

SERVES: 3 | PREP TIME: 10 MIN | COOK TIME: 5 MIN | TOTAL TIME: 15 MIN

36 large shrimp (31/35 per pound), peeled and deveined

6 tablespoons butter

1/4 cup chives

1/4 cup thinly sliced red chilies

1/4 cup chopped pickled ginger

2 tablespoons pickled ginger brine

1/4 cup gin

Sliced baguette

Melt butter in a large skillet over medium low heat. Once the butter is foaming, add the shrimp to the skillet in an even layer, followed by tablespoons of chives. Cook for 2 minutes. Flip the shrimp to cook on the other side and add the chilies, ginger, ginger brine, and gin.

Cook until shrimp are no longer translucent, about 1 more minute. Remove from heat, then top with remaining 2 tablespoons of chives.

Serve with sliced baguette.

manhattan RIBS

If bourbon BBQ sauce is good, Manhattan BBQ sauce is better. Put it on ribs, chicken, burgers, whatever you have. Having a party? Get a few mason jars and bottle the sauce for a hostess gift.

**SERVES: 4 | PREP TIME: 15 MIN | COOK TIME: 2 HRS + 40 MIN | INACTIVE TIME: 15 MIN
TOTAL TIME: 3 HRS + 10 MIN**

FOR THE MANHATTAN
- 2 ounces bourbon
- 1 ounce sweet vermouth
- 1 ounce dry vermouth

FOR THE MANHATTAN BBQ SAUCE
- 1 cup ketchup
- 1/2 cup crushed tomatoes (or tomato passata/purée)
- 1/2 cup beef stock
- 1/4 cup Worcestershire sauce
- 2 tablespoons brown coconut sugar (or light brown sugar)
- 2 tablespoons apple cider vinegar
- 1 teaspoon black pepper
- 1 tablespoon chili powder
- 1/4 cup grated onion
- 1 tablespoon garlic paste
- 1 Manhattan

FOR THE RIBS
- 2 racks baby back ribs
- 1/4 cup BBQ spice rub

MAKE THE THE MANHATTAN
Combine all ingredients in a pitcher over ice. Stir, strain and divide into 2 martini glasses, garnishing each with a maraschino cherry.

MAKE THE THE MANHATTAN BBQ SAUCE
Simmer all ingredients in a pot over medium low for 20-30 minutes, until thick.

MAKE THE THE RIBS
Preheat oven to 300F. Season baby back ribs with spice rub, front and back. Seal the racks completely in aluminum foil. Place on a baking sheet and bake for 2 hours.

Remove the ribs from the oven and fire up the BBQ. Take the foil off and let the ribs rest for 10 minutes or so.

Cut down cleanly between the bones and brush each rib with Manhattan BBQ sauce.

Grill the ribs until lightly charred, about 5 minutes per side.

Cool ribs for 5 minutes, then serve.

lamb chops WITH MOJITO CHIMICHURRI

A kicky spin on mint jelly and lamb, this preparation will make you wonder how you ever lived without boozy chimichurri.

**SERVES: 2 | PREP TIME: 15 MIN | COOK TIME: 10 MIN | INACTIVE TIME: 35 MIN
TOTAL TIME: 1 HR**

4 lamb chops

2 teaspoons salt

4 garlic cloves, skins removed and flattened/smashed

1 cup extra virgin olive oil

2/3 cup lime juice

2 tablespoons rum

1 cup mint leaves

Preheat oven to 450F.

Lightly season lamb chops with 1 teaspoon of salt.

Combine 3 garlic cloves, 1/2 cup extra virgin olive oil, 1/3 lime juice, 1 tablespoon rum, and a few mint leaves.

Marinate the lamb chops in this mixture at room temperature for 30 minutes. Discard marinade.

To make the Mojito sauce, pulse remaining garlic, olive oil, lime juice, rum, and salt in a small food processor until combined.

Preheat an oven-safe frying pan over high heat for about a minute. Carefully add the lamb chops to the pan and sear until well browned, about 2 minutes. Flip the chops and sear the other side, about 1 minute.

Carefully transfer the frying pan with the lamb chops to the oven. Roast to medium-rare (130F) or medium (135F), which should take about 3-5 minutes. Remove the chops from the oven and transfer to a plate to rest 5 minutes.

Serve with Mojito sauce.

creamy peppercorn PATTIES

Salisbury Steak grew up, met a saucy playmate, and got into some real peppery shenanigans in the galley. Cognac was blamed; all are culpable.

**SERVES: 4 | PREP TIME: 10 MIN | COOK TIME: 15 MIN | INACTIVE TIME: 5 MIN
TOTAL TIME: 30 MIN**

FOR THE PATTIES

1/2 cup grated onion

1/2 cup panko breadcrumbs

1 pound ground beef, at room temperature

1 teaspoon garlic salt

1 teaspoon mustard powder

1 beaten egg

2 tablespoons ketchup

1 teaspoon Worcestershire sauce

2 tablespoons olive oil

FOR THE PEPPERCORN SAUCE

2 tablespoons whole black peppercorns

1/4 cup cognac

1/4 cup beef stock

1/2 cup half-and-half

Chopped parsley, for garnish

MAKE THE PATTIES

Combine breadcrumbs and grated onion in a bowl. Set aside for 5 minutes to allow breadcrumbs to slightly moisten; then add ground beef, garlic salt, mustard powder, egg, ketchup, and Worcestershire.

Mix the meat mixture with your hands until slightly pasty and divide into 4 oval patties, about 1-inch thick.

Heat oil in a pan over medium high heat. When the oil shimmers, add the patties cook, without flipping, for 3-4 minutes, until browned. Flip the patties and brown the other side, another 2-3 minutes.

Remove from heat and transfer patties to a plate.

MAKE THE PEPPERCORN SAUCE

Crush the pepper using a rolling pin, mortar and pestle, or the back of a heavy pan; set aside.

Add cognac to the same pan you browned the patties and deglaze over low heat, scraping [...] may be sticking. Add the cognac and simmer for 2 minutes to reduce. Add beef stock, bring to a boil, and reduce by half, about 3-5 minutes. Reduce heat to medium. Add half-and-half and peppercorns and gently simmer for about 2 minutes, until slightly thickened.

Top patties with peppercorn sauce and garnish with chopped parsley.

orange CHICKEN

This Asian-inspired chicken delivers the citrusy flavor we love in the Chinese take-out classic, without the greasy fried coating. And now you have a use for that marmalade you bought last year. You're welcome.

SERVES: 4 | PREP TIME: 10 MIN | COOK TIME: 15 MIN | TOTAL TIME: 25 MIN

FOR THE ORANGE GLAZE

- 1/4 cup orange-flavored liqueur
- 2 tablespoons soy sauce
- 3/4 cup orange marmalade
- 2 tablespoons brown sugar
- 1/2 teaspoon minced garlic
- 1/2 teaspoon salt

FOR THE CHICKEN

- 1 teaspoon salt
- 1 teaspoon pepper
- 1 cup all-purpose flour
- 1 teaspoon garlic powder
- 1/2 teaspoon ground ginger
- 1 pound chicken breasts, cubed
- 3 tablespoons extra virgin olive oil
- 2 tablespoons toasted sesame seeds
- 1/4 cup finely chopped scallions

MAKE THE ORANGE GLAZE

In a small pot over medium low heat, combine liqueur, soy sauce, marmalade, brown sugar, garlic, and salt and cook for 5 minutes.

Set aside.

MAKE THE CHICKEN

Pat chicken with paper towels to ensure it is completely dry.

Combine flour, garlic powder, and ground ginger. Toss chicken in seasoned flour, ensuring a light dusting on all sides.

Heat olive oil in a pan over medium heat and sauté chicken until golden, about 5-8 minutes. Transfer cooked chicken to a bowl and combine with orange glaze.

Garnish with sesame seeds and scallions.

beef STROGANOFF

One of gastronomy's most notable, inclusive creations: founded by the French, created in Russia, embraced by the Chinese. A multicultural triumph!

SERVES: 4 | PREP TIME: 15 MIN | COOK TIME: 1 HR | TOTAL TIME: 1 HR + 15 MIN

- **1 pound boneless ribeye steak, thinly sliced**
- **1/4 cup flour**
- **1 1/2 teaspoons salt**
- **1 1/2 teaspoons pepper**
- **6 tablespoons unsalted butter**
- **8 ounces sliced mushrooms**
- **1/3 cup minced shallot**
- **1 teaspoon minced garlic**
- **1/4 cup brandy**
- **2 cups beef broth**
- **1 dried bay leaf**
- **2 teaspoons Dijon mustard**
- **1/2 teaspoon fresh thyme**
- **6 ounces sour cream**
- **1 tablespoon chopped parsley**
- **Egg noodles, for serving**

Pat the ribeye dry with paper towels. Place the meat in a medium bowl. Combine flour, 1 teaspoon salt, and 1 teaspoon pepper and coat the steak with the seasoned flour.

In a large pan, heat 4 tablespoons of butter over medium high heat until melted. Sear the beef until browned on all sides, about 10 minutes; transfer the beef to a plate.

Melt remaining 2 tablespoons of butter in the skillet over medium heat. Add the shallots and mushrooms and sauté, stirring frequently, for 5-7 minutes, until mushrooms are lightly browned. Add the garlic and sauté until fragrant, about 1 minute. Add the beef to the pan, as well as any accumulated juices. Add the brandy and deglaze the pan, lifting anything that may be sticking to the bottom. Reduce the brandy to 2-3 tablespoons, about 10 minutes. Add beef broth, bay leaf, mustard, thyme, 1/2 teaspoon salt, and 1/2 teaspoon pepper. Let the beef simmer, uncovered, for 30 minutes, until very tender. Discard the bay leaf. Add sour cream, reduce heat to low, and simmer for 2 minutes.

Garnish with parsley and serve over noodles.

sides

NEXT UP, TEN SIDE DISHES THAT WILL COME TO YOUR RESCUE FOR POTLUCKS, SHOWERS, AND LAST-MINUTE DINNER GUESTS.

Some baked sides, some stove-top creations, and at least one dish that will look awfully familiar from the Appetizer chapter. Hint: you'll learn how shake up Swiss Fondue to make a whimsical riff on macaroni and cheese, called Mac & 'Due (p. 92). And while we're switching things up, swap out the onion jam, thyme, and Gruyère filling in the French Onion Crostata for Spinach Rockefeller (p. 84). Two sides in one!

PROST!

mac & due

Mac and cheese is cool—but Mac and [Fon]Due is cooler! This recipe takes Swiss Fondue (p. 25) from the bunny slopes to the black-diamond run. Better yet, skip the mountain and head to the lodge. Your bowl of joy is waiting.

SERVES: 4 | PREP TIME: 5 MIN | COOK TIME: 32 MIN | TOTAL TIME: 37 MIN

- 8 ounces Italian sausage, casings removed
- 1 pound ditalini
- 1 1/2 tablespoons butter
- 1 1/2 tablespoons flour
- 2 teaspoons kirsch
- 1/4 cup dry white wine
- 3/4 cup milk
- 1/2 teaspoon salt
- 1/2 teaspoon pepper
- 2 cups grated Emmental
- 2 cups grated Gruyère
- 4 ounces chopped cornichon
- 1/4 cup onion jam
- 1 cup halved, seedless grapes
- 1/4 cup chopped chives, for garnish

Preheat oven to 400F.

Roll Italian sausage into balls, about 1/2-ounce each. Place sausage balls on a parchment-lined baking sheet and roast until cooked through, about 12-15 minutes. Allow sausage balls to cool; set aside.

Cook ditalini according to package instructions, about 10 minutes. Reserve 1/2 cup of starchy cooking water. Drain pasta; set aside.

In a small saucepan, melt butter over medium-high heat. Once foaming, add flour and whisk until slightly golden, about 1 minute. Whisking constantly, slowly add kirsch, wine, and milk until all ingredients are well incorporated, about 3 minutes. Add salt and pepper and reduce heat to low, stirring frequently. Add Emmental and Gruyere and continue to cook until thickened, about 2-3 more minutes. Combine cooked ditalini and cheese sauce. If the sauce is too thick, add reserved pasta water, 1 tablespoon at a time, until desired consistency is achieved.

Add cornichon, onion jam, grapes, and sausage balls to the pasta and serve, garnished with chives.

sloppy PEAS

I know what you're thinking—this is not the same as Split Pea Soup. That said, if you have a lot of time on your hands, and have dried marrowfat peas, Sloppy Peas are a spectacular vegan alternative to its ham-laden look-a-like. And, they're dynamite next to a steak. (Omit the steak for vegans.)

**SERVES: 4 | PREP TIME: 10 MIN | COOK TIME: 35 MIN | INACTIVE TIME: 12 HRS
TOTAL TIME: 12 HRS + 45 MIN**

6 cups water

2 teaspoons baking soda

9 ounces dried marrowfat peas

3 tablespoons gin

Bring 3 cups of water to a boil. Dissolve the baking soda in boiling water.

Place the peas in a bowl and cover with the boiling water. Stir peas and set aside to soak for at least 12 hours.

Drain the peas, rinse them thoroughly, and transfer them to a pot with remaining 3 cups of water.

Bring peas to a boil, cover, reduce heat to medium-low and cook for 30 minutes, stirring occasionally, until peas have completely broken down. Remove cover, add gin, increase heat to medium and cook an additional 10 minutes.

spinach ROCKEFELLER

Everybody knows that in Oysters Rockefeller, all the good stuff is baked on top. Who needs the oysters? Let's cut out the middle-mollusk. It's all about efficiency.

SERVES: 4 | PREP TIME: 15 MIN | COOK TIME: 30 MIN | INACTIVE TIME: 15 MIN
TOTAL TIME: 1 HR

6 tablespoons unsalted butter

2 teaspoons minced garlic

1 cup Panko breadcrumbs

1/4 cup minced shallots

4 cups frozen spinach, thawed and excess water removed

1/4 cup anise-flavored liqueur

1 teaspoon salt

2 tablespoons black pepper

1/2 teaspoon hot sauce

2 tablespoons lemon juice

2 tablespoons chopped chervil

2 tablespoons olive oil

1/2 cup grated Parmesan

Lemon wedges, for serving

Preheat oven to 400F.

In a large skillet over medium low, add the butter and garlic. Sauté the garlic for 1 minute, until fragrant.

Transfer half of the garlic butter to a bowl and add the breadcrumbs, olive oil, Parmesan, and chervil. Mix to combine; set aside.

To the remaining garlic butter in the skillet, add shallots and spinach, cook for 3 minutes until the spinach wilts. Deglaze the pan with liqueur. Add salt, pepper, hot sauce, and lemon juice and continue cooking for 3 more minutes.

Transfer spinach mixture to a baking dish; top with breadcrumb mixture, and bake for 20 minutes until golden.

Serve with lemon wedges.

french onion CROSTATA

Onion jam, brandy, thyme leaves, and shredded Gruyère, baked in a flat pie crust. A pinch of flaky salt on the egg-washed pie dough ensures flavorful, golden, flake-itude!

**SERVES: 4 | PREP TIME: 5 MIN | COOK TIME: 25 MIN | INACTIVE TIME: 15 MIN
TOTAL TIME: 45 MIN**

1 refrigerated, rolled pie crust

1/3 cup onion jam

2 tablespoons brandy

1 teaspoon thyme

3 ounces grated Gruyère

Preheat oven to 400F.

Unroll the pie dough.

Combine onion jam and brandy. Spread onion mixture on the pie dough leaving a 1-inch border. Sprinkle thyme over onion mixture, followed by Gruyère.

Turn up the dough and pinch every couple inches to enclose the filling. Brush the exposed pie dough with egg wash and sprinkle the egg wash with a little flaky salt.

Bake until golden, about 20-25 minutes.

Cool on a wire rack for 10-15 minutes before serving.

cranberry SAUCE

Thanksgiving's trusty side is phenomenal on sandwiches, sensational over vanilla ice cream, and downright dangerous when dolloped on braised greens.

SERVES: 6 | PREP TIME: 5 MIN | COOK TIME: 30 MIN | TOTAL TIME: 35 MIN

12 ounces frozen cranberries, thawed

1 1/2 cups sugar

1 green apple, peeled, cored and diced

1 tablespoon orange zest

1/2 cup orange juice

1/2 teaspoon grated ginger

1 tablespoon orange liqueur

In a medium pot over low heat, combine all ingredients with 1/2 cup of water. Cook until the cranberries are mostly broken down, about 30 minutes.

Remove from the heat, cool, and serve room temperature.

lentilles FRANÇAISES

Basic grocery store lentils, elegantly prepared. Need a little more foo-foo? Eat with your pinky up. Bon appétit!

SERVES: 4　|　PREP TIME: 5 MIN　|　COOK TIME: 25 MIN　|　TOTAL TIME: 30 MIN

1 cup dried brown lentils

3 cups vegetable broth

1 tablespoon butter

1/2 cup minced shallots

1 tablespoon cognac

3 tablespoons chopped fresh flat-leaf parsley

1 teaspoon fresh thyme leaves

1/2 teaspoon salt

1/2 teaspoon pepper

Place lentils and broth in a pot over high heat and bring to a boil. Reduce heat to medium low, and simmer 20-25 minutes, until lentils are tender. Drain lentils and set aside.

Melt butter in a large skillet over medium heat. Once butter is foaming, sauté shallots for 2 minutes. Add cognac and cook an additional minute. Add cooked lentils, parsley, thyme, salt and pepper.

Stir to combine.

fennel cutlets AND ORANGE DIPPING SAUCE

I created this recipe because it occurred to me that, aside from fried green tomatoes and eggplant parmesan, vegetarians aren't getting enough breading. Plus, I figured you'd be looking for more reasons to use your anise-flavored liqueur. I got you.

SERVES: 3 | PREP TIME: 15 MIN | COOK TIME: 30 MIN | TOTAL TIME: 45 MIN

FOR THE ORANGE DIPPING SAUCE

- 1 cup mayonnaise
- 2 tablespoons orange juice
- 2 tablespoons anise-flavored liqueur

FOR THE FENNEL

- 6 1/2-inch fennel steaks (about 2 fennel bulbs, tops removed and sliced lengthwise)
- 1 cup all-purpose flour
- 1/2 cup cornstarch
- 1 teaspoon poultry seasoning
- 2 beaten eggs
- 2 teaspoons anise-flavored liqueur
- 1 cup breadcrumbs
- 1 cup grated Parmesan cheese
- 1 cup vegetable oil
- 2 teaspoons salt

MAKE THE ORANGE SAUCE
Combine all ingredients and refrigerate until serving.

MAKE THE FENNEL
Add fennel to a large pot and cover with water. Bring to a boil over high heat and cook fennel until slightly tender, 6-8 minutes. Drain the fennel and cool. Pat fennel dry with paper towels and sprinkle with 1 teaspoon salt.

In a medium bowl, combine cornstarch, flour, and poultry seasoning. In a second medium bowl, combine eggs and liqueur. In a third medium bowl, combine breadcrumbs and Parmesan. Dust the first fennel cutlet in the seasoned flour, then coat with the egg mixture, allowing any excess to drip back in to the bowl. Coat the fennel cutlet in the breadcrumb mixture on both sides, pressing down on the fennel to ensure the coating sticks. Repeat to bread the remaining fennel cutlets.

In a large pot over medium heat, add the vegetable oil. When the oil reaches 350F, carefully place 3 cutlets in the pot and fry, undisturbed, until golden, 1-2 minutes. Flip the cutlets over to brown the other side, about 1-2 more minutes. Repeat to fry remaining fennel cutlets.

Season cutlets with remaining 1 teaspoon of salt and serve with orange dipping sauce.

maple bourbon SWEET POTATOES

In the absence of sweet potatoes, this maple-pumpkin pie spice-bourbon combo makes an epic cocktail. Toddy it up! (Mental note: Add sweet potatoes to the grocery list. Oh, and maybe some chopped pecans to sprinkle on top.)

SERVES: 4 | PREP TIME: 10 MIN | COOK TIME: 12 MIN | TOTAL TIME: 22 MIN

- 1 pound sweet potatoes, peeled and cut into 1-inch pieces
- 1 1/2 cups water
- 1 1/2 teaspoons salt
- 2 tablespoons unsalted butter
- 1/2 teaspoon pumpkin pie spice
- 1 teaspoon maple syrup
- 1 tablespoon bourbon

Insert the metal trivet into the inner cooking pot of a multicooker. Place the sweet potatoes on the trivet. Some sweet potatoes may fall through to the bottom. Add water and 1 teaspoon of salt. Secure the lid, select pressure cook or manual mode, and set timer for 12 minutes.

Using a towel to protect your hand, "quick release" the pressure by turning the steam release handle on the lid to the "venting" position. Remove the lid and using hot pads, carefully remove the inner cooking pot, drain the sweet potatoes, and transfer the sweet potatoes to a large bowl.

Add butter, pumpkin pie spice, remaining 1/2 teaspoon salt, maple syrup and bourbon to the sweet potatoes and mash until smooth.

mushrooms BORRACHOS

Buttery, browned mushrooms and earthy tequila are a dreamy combination. Slather them on steaks. Tuck them into omelets. Stir them into fondue. Top them on your Cream of Mushroom Soup (p. 48). Swirl them into risotto. Olé!

SERVES: 2 | PREP TIME: 5 MIN | COOK TIME: 15 MIN | TOTAL TIME: 20 MIN

2 tablespoons butter

8 ounces sliced mushrooms

1/4 teaspoon salt

1/4 cup tequila

Melt 1 tablespoon of butter in a large nonstick skillet over medium-high heat. Add the mushrooms to the skillet, and stir to coat the mushrooms in the butter. Add salt and spread the mushrooms in an even layer across the pan. Cook the mushrooms, undisturbed, until brown on the bottom, about 5 minutes.

Flip the mushrooms to brown on the other side, another 2-3 minutes, without stirring. Deglaze with tequila and cook for another 2-3 minutes, until the tequila reduces slightly. Add remaining tablespoon of butter and reduce another 1-2 minutes.

risotto INVERNO

Pasta Primavera is so 80s. This wintery risotto spin takes some help from the store with frozen root vegetables... and gin!

SERVES: 4 | PREP TIME: 10 MIN | COOK TIME: 40 MIN | TOTAL TIME: 50 MIN

- 6 cups vegetable broth
- 3 tablespoons extra virgin olive oil
- 1/2 cup minced onion
- 2 cups arborio rice
- 1/4 cup gin
- 1 pound frozen diced, fully cooked root vegetables, thawed
- 2 tablespoons butter
- 1/2 cup grated Parmesan cheese

In a pot over medium heat, warm the broth.

In a large, heavy saucepan, heat the oil over medium heat. Add onion and sauté until softened, about 4 minutes. Add rice and coat every grain in the oil. Toast rice for about 3 minutes, until you can see a white dot in each grain, about 3 minutes. Add gin and stir until it's absorbed. Once absorbed, add broth, about a half cup at a time, stirring frequently, as it's absorbed into the rice.

Reserve about 1/4 cup of broth.

When the rice is tender and creamy, after about 20 minutes, stir in the root vegetables. Heat through, about 1-2 minutes. Remove risotto from heat and stir in the butter, Parmesan, and remaining broth.

Season with salt and pepper, as needed.

desserts

FANCY CONFECTIONS CAN BE INTIMIDATING, BUT HAVE NO FEAR. Six of the 10 recipes in this chapter are simple, no-bake, lip-smacking desserts that are a breeze to prepare! And there are plenty of unexpected tips in the remaining pages as well. For example, you'll learn that melted vanilla ice cream with a smidge of rum makes the perfect sauce for bread pudding. Speaking of vanilla ice cream, how about a boozy shake? A Black Russian and a White Russian walk into a bar and… well, you'll see.

À VOTRE SANTÉ!

currant challah pudding
WITH CRÈME ANG**LAZY**

Pillowy challah and dried currants are an amazing shake-up to raisin bread pudding. And did you know that the luscious dessert cream sauce, called crème anglaise, is basically melted vanilla ice cream with a couple of egg yolks? Skip the yolks, add a tablespoon of rum, et voilà!!

SERVES: 4 | PREP TIME: 10 MIN | COOK TIME: 35 MIN | INACTIVE TIME: 15 MIN
TOTAL TIME: 1 HR

FOR THE CURRANT CHALLAH PUDDING

- Non-stick cooking spray
- 1/4 cup brown sugar
- 1 cup milk
- 2 tablespoons rum
- 3 eggs
- 1/2 teaspoon cinnamon
- 1/4 teaspoon salt
- 1/3 cup dried currants
- 2 cups challah, cut into 1-inch cubes

FOR THE CRÈME ANGLAZY

- 1/3 cup vanilla ice cream, softened
- 2 teaspoons rum
- 1/4 teaspoon salt

MAKE THE CRÈME ANGLAZY

Add ice cream, rum, and salt to a small pot. Allow mixture simmer for 3 minutes. Remove from heat and set aside.

MAKE THE CURRANT CHALLAH PUDDING

Preheat the oven to 375F.

Generously coat an 8x8" baking dish with cooking spray.

In a large mixing bowl combine the sugar, milk, rum, eggs, cinnamon, and salt. Use a whisk to thoroughly mix. Add the cubes of challah to the mixture and toss to evenly coat. Fold in the currants and pour the mixture into the prepared pan.

Bake for 30 to 40 minutes or until the bread pudding has puffed up and is golden brown along the edges.

Cool bread pudding on a wire rack for 15 minutes.

Serve with a generous drizzle of Crème angLazy.

amaretti

If you've ever had a crispy, crumbly Italian cookie wrapped in distinctive, bright paper, pulled from a persimmon-colored tin, you've had a version of these. Let's give them a run for their money.

**MAKES 24 COOKIES | PREP TIME: 15 MIN | COOK TIME: 30 MIN | INACTIVE TIME: 15 MIN
TOTAL TIME: 1 HR**

- 2 1/4 cups finely milled almond flour
- 1 cup granulated sugar
- 1/4 teaspoon salt
- 2 large egg whites
- 1/4 teaspoon lemon juice
- 1 teaspoon amaretto liqueur
- 3 tablespoons powdered sugar

Preheat oven to 300 F.

In a large bowl, combine almond flour, sugar, and salt until evenly incorporated; set aside. Add egg whites and lemon juice to a bowl and whisk vigorously (or whip using an electric mixer) until soft peaks form.

Add beaten egg whites and amaretto to the dry ingredients and stir until a soft, sticky dough forms.

Compress about 1-2 teaspoons of dough into a ball (about 20-24 cookies), and arrange on a parchment-lined baking sheet.

Bake for 30 minutes until the cookie tops are cracked and their bottoms are golden.

Transfer cookies to a cooling rack for 15 minutes, then dust with powdered sugar before serving.

chocolate hazelnut "MOUSSE"

It looks like mousse—but it's quicker, smarter, and downright tastier than the original. And no pesky whipped egg whites. I know. Genius.

SERVES: 4 | PREP TIME: 5 MIN | INACTIVE TIME: 1 HR | TOTAL TIME: 1 HR + 5 MIN

- **1 cup sweetened hazelnut cocoa spread**
- **2 cups frozen whipped topping, thawed**
- **1/4 cup hazelnut liqueur**
- **2 tablespoons mini chocolate chips, for serving**

Using an electric mixer, combine hazelnut spread, whipped topping, and liqueur until well incorporated, about 1-2 minutes.

Chill for a minimum of 1 hour and serve with a sprinkle of mini chocolate chips.

blackberry CLAFOUTIS

This dessert could just has easily have been called [Insert Fruit Here] Clafoutis. The first version I learned to make was pear and brandy—good, but not nearly as creamy and comforting as this. I added blackberry preserve for sweetness, smoothness, and most importantly, a velvety bed for the crème de cassis.

**SERVES: 8 | PREP TIME: 10 MIN | COOK TIME: 35 MIN | INACTIVE TIME: 10 MIN
TOTAL TIME: 55 MIN**

Nonstick cooking spray

1/3 cup plus 1 tablespoon sugar

3 eggs, at room temperature

6 tablespoons all-purpose flour

1 1/2 cups heavy cream

2 teaspoons pure vanilla extract

1 teaspoon lemon zest

1/4 teaspoon kosher salt

2 tablespoons crème de cassis

6 ounces blackberries

1/4 cup blackberry preserves

1/4 cup powdered sugar

Mint leaves, for garnish

Preheat the oven to 375 degrees F.

Apply a thin layer of nonstick cooking spray to a 10-inch round baking dish. Sprinkle the bottom and sides of the dish with 1 tablespoon of the sugar.

Using an electric mixer, beat the eggs and the 1/3 cup of sugar until light and fluffy, about 3 minutes. Slowly add the flour, cream, vanilla extract, lemon zest, and salt and mix until well incorporated. Rest the batter for 10 minutes.

In a small bowl, combine crème de cassis, blackberries, and preserves. Slightly mash the blackberries, transfer mixture to the baking dish, and spread into an even layer. Pour the batter over the blackberry mixture.

Bake for 35 minutes, until the top is golden brown and the custard is firm.

To serve, sprinkle with powdered sugar and garnish with mint.

piña colada PANNA COTTA

Italian flan, but better. No sticky caramel, and no oven required. Traditionally prepared with heavy cream and berries, this version has an island flair, complete with a rum-pineapple tiara. Yeah, mon!

SERVES: 4 | PREP TIME: 15 MIN | COOK TIME: 3 MIN | INACTIVE TIME: 2HRS + 5 MIN
TOTAL TIME: 2 HRS + 23 MIN

- 1 ½ cups crème fraiche
- 2/3 cup coconut milk
- ½ cup + 1 tablespoon sugar
- 1 ½ teaspoon unflavored gelatin powder
- 1 cup fresh pineapple, finely diced
- 2 tablespoons coconut rum
- 1 teaspoon lime zest
- ¼ cup toasted coconut
- 1 tablespoon fresh mint, shredded

To bloom the powdered gelatin, place a tablespoon of cold water in a shallow bowl. Sprinkle the gelatin evenly over the top of the water and let the mixture stand for 5 minutes.

Combine crème fraiche, coconut milk, and ½ cup of sugar in a pot over medium heat. Bring to a boil and remove from the heat. Stir in bloomed gelatin and whisk well until gelatin is completely incorporated and smooth.

Pour the mixture into four ramekins and refrigerate for at least 2 hours.

Add pineapple, 1 tablespoon sugar, and rum and cook over medium heat for 3 minutes. Transfer pineapple mixture to a bowl, add lime zest, and cool.

When ready to serve, top panna cotta with pineapple mixture and garnish with toasted coconut and mint.

russian SHAKE

Black Russians and White Russians are exactly the same, except for a little dairy in the latter. After some well-needed therapy in the blender, they are no longer on the rocks. Diversity makes everything better.

SERVES: 2 | PREP TIME: 10 MIN | TOTAL TIME: 10 MIN

1 1/2 cups ice

1 cup vanilla ice cream

1/2 cup milk

4 ounces vodka

2 ounces coffee liqueur

Combine all ingredients in a blender. Cover and pulse until the mixture starts to combine. Blend on high until completely smooth, about 15-20 seconds.

limoncello TRIFLE

Breaking news! Angel food cake and limoncello co-anchor this crack team of lemony go-getters. Tartness from the lemon juice, sweetness from the lemon pie filling. Fair and balanced, as it should be.

SERVES: 10 | PREP TIME: 15 MIN | INACTIVE TIME 2 HRS | TOTAL TIME: 2 HRS + 15 MIN

8 ounces vanilla wafer cookies

8 ounces plain angel food cake, cubed

1/2 cup limoncello

1 22-ounce can lemon pie filling, lemon curd, or lemon pudding

12 ounces frozen whipped topping, thawed

4 teaspoons lemon juice

1 tablespoon lemon zest

Yellow gum drops

Crush 3 vanilla wafers and place the crumbs in a small bowl; set aside.

Add cake and limoncello to a medium bowl. Gently press the cake to absorb all the limoncello. Place half the moistened cake in the bottom of a deep glass bowl, followed by half of the pie filling.

Combine whipped topping, lemon juice, and 1 tablespoon of lemon zest. Place half of the lemon whipped topping mixture on top of the pie filling.

Stand a layer of cookies vertically against the perimeter of the bowl, so you see the cookies along the edge of the glass dish. Place some vanilla wafers on top of the lemon whipped topping, then add the remainder off the cake, followed by the remainder of the pie filling, then the lemon whipped topping.

Stand another layer of cookies vertically against the perimeter of the bowl. Garnish the top of the trifle with remaining lemon zest, vanilla wafer crumbs, and gum drops.

Refrigerate trifle for at least two hours before serving.

cannoli TIRAMISU

A mashup of two legendary desserts, this method can be adapted in numerous ways to suit your taste. Can't find Italian cocktail cherries? Mix ¼ cup of cherry preserves with frozen sweet cherries.

SERVES: 6 | PREP TIME: 15 MIN | INACTIVE TIME: 3 HRS | TOTAL TIME: 3 HRS + 15 MIN

1 cup whole milk ricotta

1 cup heavy cream

2 ounces simple syrup

2 ounces cherry liqueur

7 ounces ladyfingers (about 24, total)

14 ounces Italian cocktail cherries in marasca syrup

1 cup chopped pistachios

1 cup chocolate chips

Using an electric mixer, mix ricotta and cream for 1 minute until well combined.

Combine simple syrup and cherry liqueur in a shallow dish. Lightly dip half of the ladyfingers in the liqueur mixture and line them up side by side across the bottom of an 8x8-inch pan.

Pour half of the ricotta mixture on top of the ladyfingers. Sprinkle half the cherries, pistachios, and chocolate over the ricotta mixture.

Dip the remaining ladyfingers in the liqueur mixture and repeat to create a second layer over the cherries, pistachios, and chocolate.

Top ladyfingers with remaining ricotta mixture, then garnish with remaining cherries, pistachios, and chocolate.

Cover and refrigerate for at least 3 hours.

To serve, drizzle a little marasca syrup (from the jar) on top.

mudslide PIE

Suggestion: Make a couple extra mudslides to get through the seven hours of freeze time this pie needs to reach its chocolaty glory. Then rejoice as you and five friends melt into a puddle of bliss!

**SERVES: 6 | PREP TIME: 20 MIN | COOK TIME: 1 MIN | INACTIVE TIME: 6 HR + 30 MIN
TOTAL TIME: 7 HR**

- 1 6-ounce chocolate cookie crumb crust
- 2 cups coffee ice cream, softened
- 2 ounces vodka
- 2 ounces coffee liqueur
- 3 ounces Irish cream liqueur
- 3 ounces heavy cream
- 8 ounces miniature chocolate chips
- 12 ounces jarred hot fudge
- 8 chocolate sandwich cookies, crushed
- 8 ounces whipped topping, thawed
- Chocolate shavings

Freeze the crust for 30 minutes, until firm.

In a large bowl, combine ice cream, vodka, liqueurs, and heavy cream. Place half of the mixture in a separate bowl and stir in the chocolate chips. Place chocolate chip mixture in the freezer.

Remove the crust from the freezer. Spread the ice cream mixture in an even layer over the frozen crust; then freeze for 2 hours.

Microwave the fudge topping for 30-60 seconds until pourable. Reserve 2 tablespoons of cookie crumbs in a small bowl and add remaining cookie crumbs to the fudge topping. Remove the pie from the freezer and add the fudge in an even layer. Return to freezer for 2 hours.

Take the chocolate chip ice cream mixture out of the freezer and allow to stand for about 10 minutes to soften. Remove pie from the freezer and layer the remaining ice cream mixture over the layer of cookie crumbs and fudge topping. Cover with plastic wrap, and return to freezer for 2 more hours.

Remove pie, and frost the top of the pie with the whipped topping. Cover with plastic wrap, and return to freezer for 2 more hours to freeze the whipped topping layer.

When ready to serve, garnish pie with reserved cookie crumbs and chocolate shavings.

sabayune

AKA zabaglione in some Italian regions, this luscious dessert is lighter than a pudding, but richer than a sauce. Adorned with frozen, Marsala-soaked grapes, it's a feast for the senses, as well as the palate.

SERVES: 4 | PREP TIME: 10 MIN | COOK TIME: 6 MIN | INACTIVE TIME: 2 HR
TOTAL TIME: 2 HR + 16 MIN

1 1/2 cup Marsala

1/3 cup chopped seedless grapes

8 egg yolks

1 1/2 cups granulated sugar

Combine 1/4 cup Marsala and grapes and freeze for a minimum of 2 hours.

In a heat-safe bowl, whisk yolks and sugar until the mixture becomes a light yellow, about 1 minute. Stir in Marsala.

Place the bowl over a pot of simmering water, making sure the water does not touch the bottom of the bowl. Gently whisk the mixture until thickened, about 5 minutes. Remove bowl from the heat and transfer sabayune to stemmed glasses or bowls.

Refrigerate for a minimum of 2 hours before serving.

Copyright © 2023

NAMES:
Shevetone, Alicia, author.

TITLE:
Food with Spirit / Alicia Shevetone

BOOK + COVER DESIGN:
April Hennessey

EDITOR:
Traci Keller

COVER PHOTOGRAPHY:
David Sadleir

FIRST EDITION

About the Author

Alicia Shevetone is an author, culinary personality, and pop-up chef. An expert in the development of recipes for two, her breakout cookbook, *Italian Cookbook for Two*, celebrates her Northern Italian heritage and exposes readers to a side of Italian food they don't normally experience. Her second cookbook, *Vegetarian Ketogenic Cookbook for Beginners*, showcases 75 savory, low-carb, plant-based recipes that anyone can master to maintain a healthy lifestyle.

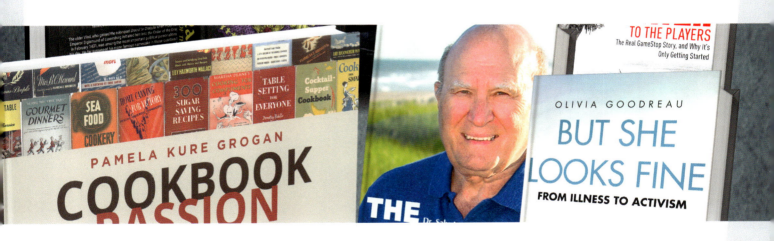

GAUDIUM PUBLISHING

Books to challenge and enlighten
For these and other great books visit

HISTRIABOOKS.COM